YOUR KNOWLEDGE HAS VALUE

- We will publish your bachelor's and master's thesis, essays and papers

- Your own eBook and book - sold worldwide in all relevant shops

- Earn money with each sale

Upload your text at www.GRIN.com
and publish for free

Bibliographic information published by the German National Library:

The German National Library lists this publication in the National Bibliography; detailed bibliographic data are available on the Internet at http://dnb.dnb.de .

This book is copyright material and must not be copied, reproduced, transferred, distributed, leased, licensed or publicly performed or used in any way except as specifically permitted in writing by the publishers, as allowed under the terms and conditions under which it was purchased or as strictly permitted by applicable copyright law. Any unauthorized distribution or use of this text may be a direct infringement of the author s and publisher s rights and those responsible may be liable in law accordingly.

Imprint:

Copyright © 2014 GRIN Verlag, Open Publishing GmbH
Print and binding: Books on Demand GmbH, Norderstedt Germany
ISBN: 978-3-668-04025-0

This book at GRIN:

http://www.grin.com/en/e-book/305983/the-german-wirtschaftswunder-an-economic-miracle

Bikal Dhungel

The German Wirtschaftswunder. An Economic Miracle

How Germany Developed after World War II

GRIN Publishing

GRIN - Your knowledge has value

Since its foundation in 1998, GRIN has specialized in publishing academic texts by students, college teachers and other academics as e-book and printed book. The website www.grin.com is an ideal platform for presenting term papers, final papers, scientific essays, dissertations and specialist books.

Visit us on the internet:

http://www.grin.com/

http://www.facebook.com/grincom

http://www.twitter.com/grin_com

Contents

1) Introduction — 2

2) World War II and Before — 2

3) German Economic Growth — 3

4) Marshall Plan and Recovery — 4

5) Role of Institutions and Geography — 5

6) Conclusion — 6

Tables

Appendix

References

1) Introduction:

This Essay will deal about the story of economic growth of post-World War-II Germany. Devastated in terms of material loss and human well-being, Germany puts its name in the books of Economic History as a success story of development. The 'Wirtschaftswunder' (Economic Miracle) that started in early 50s is a matter of topic that has been intensely studied by scholars. The Essay will briefly describe some facts prior to World War II and the extent of loss during the war. The following part will highlight some data about the growth and explain how this was achieved and finally conclude everything.

2) World War II and Before:

It is worth noting that pre-World War I Germany was already among the wealthiest countries in the world (3rd largest in 1913) (Madison) with high level of industrialization. Already in 1900, German economy was the largest in Europe. However, the consequences of World War I, followed by high, 'unfair' reparation payment (Keynes, 1920) and economic hardships posed serious challenges, which (as Keynes) gave rise to radicalism that eventually led to World War II. Moreover, protective tariffs imposed by foreign countries on German goods (Castillo, 2003) impaired growth. It took until 1927 for German economy to reach the level of 1913(Madison).

Even if the War Economy grew until 1944, World War II caused a huge loss of 8 million Germans including civilian deaths and other economic consequences in the following years. The opportunity cost was immeasurable. Germany also faced a breakdown of production to about one half of pre-war levels (Smolny, 1999). With already 5 million internally displaced people, other 14 million arrived from lost territories that were previously part of Germany (Oltmer, 2005). In 1946, GDP fell to the level of year 1897 (Madison), a 49 years low and comprised of only one third of the level of 1944 when the GDP was highest despite the war. This implies the huge extent of destruction.

3) German Economic Growth:

The determinants of growth will be included in the next part. This part is dedicated to the extent of growth. Figure 1 shows that Germany grew at an average of 6.55% from 1949 to 1973 and with 2.31% per year from 1974 to 1990. The year 1973/74 was hit by an Oil embargo and the German economy contracted by 1.5% while the inflation reached 7%. One can say that the 'Steady State' was reached by 1973. However, in 1967 there was also a moderate Recession which can be attributed to lower public and private investment in the previous years (Borowski, 2002). Also an Oil Embargo of 1967 following the 'Six-Day War' worsened the situation.

The Gross Capital Formation increased with an average of 7.63% per year from 1950 to 1973 and by 1% average from 1974 to 1990 (Figure 2). After the unification, until 1999, average growth slowed even further. The worker productivity increased by 5.05% from1950-70 and 2.95% from 1971-80 (Figure 3). This implies that, as Solow Model explains, growth is strongly correlated with investment and productivity in this case. From these figures we can conclude that Germany reached its steady state around 1974. After that, investment on capital averaged 1% while growth averaged 2.31% justifying the Solow Model to be correct in the case of Germany.

Figure 3 also shows the growth of real wages from 1951-80. Wages rise when productivity grows. This is one of the most important determinants of economic growth and in the case of Germany, it was partly due to the movement of labour from agricultural sector to industries (Eichengreen, 2008). The share of employment in agriculture decreased from 24.6% in 1950 to 6.8% in 1974 whereas production and service sector respectively increased from 42.9% to 44% and 32.5% to 49.1% at the same period (FSD, 2014)

4) Marshall Plan and Recovery: (How economic growth was achieved)

Following World War II, the US secretary of state, George Marshall proposed the idea of ' Marshall Plan' to rebuild European states. Along with other European countries, Germany received a substantial amount of $1.45 billion, equivalent to 14.5 billion of 2006 dollars (Williamson, 2014). Marshall fund played an important role to reinstall basic infra-structures that were crucial to stimulate growth. The effect of 'Big Push' by Marshall Fund (Figure 2) was huge.

The economic policy of newly appointed finance minister and later chancellor Dr. Ludwig Erhard stimulated a take-off. He reformed the currency from 'Reichmark' to German Mark. The new currency was devalued at the initial phase which gave a boost in exports by increasing competitive advantage. German mark slowly appreciated in mid 50s increasing the purchasing power of workers. Consequently, it gave rise to tourism industries and 'life-style economy' as the Germans became able to save a part of their earnings. One of the German strengths in the early 20th century, the Auto-mobile industry experienced a sharp rise in production level. By mid 50s, all of car industries that existed in pre-WWII period were continuing their operation (Abelshauser, 2005). Other than Automobile, machineries, electric goods and chemical industries grew rapidly and were able to boost their export. Figure-4 shows that from 1953, Germany started with a trade surplus of 1 billion which reached 24 billion in 1974 and today (2013) it stands at 194 billion. According to Madison tables, even though German growth accelerated after these reforms took place, it took until 1956/57 to reach the GDP level of 1944.

5) Institutions and Geography

The role of institutions in economic growth is vital. They are the rules of the game in a society. Prevailing economic institutions affects distribution of resources (Acemoglu et al 2005). The development of institutions like European Payment Union to liberalize trade, establishment of the central bank called ' Bundesbank ' to maintain currency stability and a subsequent law which allows it to oversee other credit institutions was enforced. It is equally indisputable that trade increases employment and it was also the case with Germany. Undisciplined financial sector can either downplay their role in growth process or put the whole economy in risk. Hence, the Bundesbank played an important role to maintain this stability. The necessity of monitoring financial institutions was reflected by the Recession of 2008. Moreover, Frankfurt am Main was made a financial hub with 'Bundesbank' itself having its head office there. The role of financial markets in economic growth is undeniable. These institutions along with the establishment of GATT and Bretton Woods system added huge contribution to the recovery after war (Eichengreen, 1992) and accelerated growth. The banking system that was already well established in the previous century had difficulties to emerge again after World War II as the chief executives of important banks were tried for their involvement in war crimes. However, the 'big banks act' of 1953 allowed the re-establishment of them (Detzer et al, 2013). Cartel Office was established to prevent the formation of business cartels and monopolies. One uniqueness of German financial system are the 'Sparkassen'/Saving Associations, a non-state institutions which run under public law that not only lends to the middle class, but also support in sustainable development in a responsible way (Simpson, 2013) Their role in helping the economy grow is immense.

German growth should also be attributed to favourable geography and climate where it has an enormous advantage. It has a seaport in the North See and the Baltic ocean. The navigable rivers like Rhein-Main originating from the Alps going through major cities in south-west and ending in North see in the Netherlands supports internal trade. North eastern part is covered by river Elbe that originates in Austria-Czech Republic and ends in North See. The transportation linkages with railway tracks and roads were/are exceptionally good. Moreover, Germany borders with 9 countries giving itself a huge advantage to trade. The most important form of energy used that time was Coal and as Germany had a huge reserve of coal, it supported the industries.

High male-mortality in the war was balanced by immigration (returning soldiers and refugees) (Carlin,2014) which stopped when Berlin Wall was built in 1961. But the process of recruiting from abroad called 'Gastarbeiterabkommen/Guestworker Pact' offset this.

6) Conclusion

The growth of Germany cannot be attributed to a single factor. It was a mix of all factors, Marshall Fund, Capital growth, Technology, Population, Institutions, Savings and favourable geography. The role of human capital (Health and Education) played an important role as well. Germany has a tendency of free education and universal healthcare with mixed system that at least guaranteed the access to everybody. This ensured the supply of highly educated and well trained healthy workforces. The model of 'Social Market Economy' also proved its sustainable capability and was successful in gaining trust, recognition and support from German people which, as a result, increased the welfare of people and increased real wage by four times from 1950 to 1980 (Haupt, 2014) and because of such policies and their further development, Germany stands as one of the wealthiest nations today.

FIGURES

Figure 1 (Source: Abelshauser 2005 Paper)

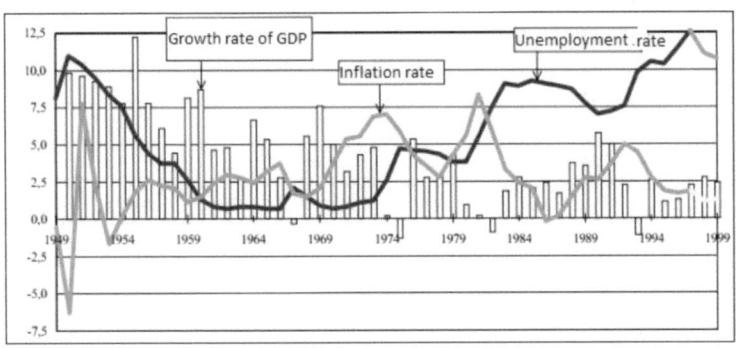

Figure 2 (Source: University of Munich, Center for Macroeconomic Studies)

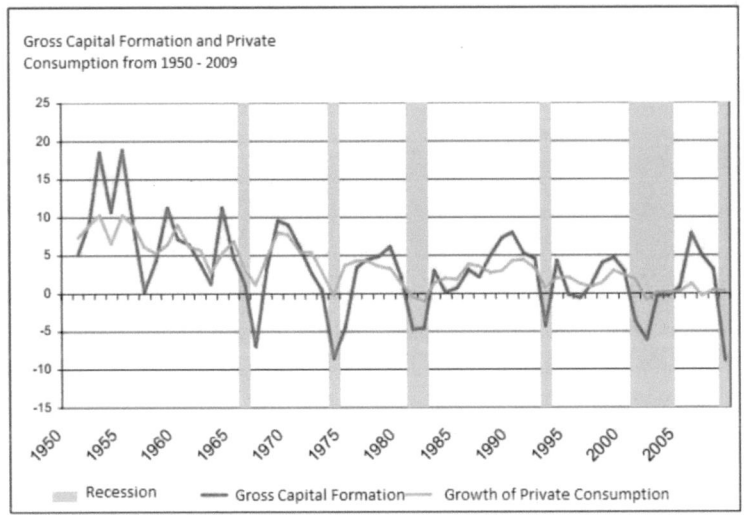

Figure 3 (Source: Federal Statistical Office, 2014)

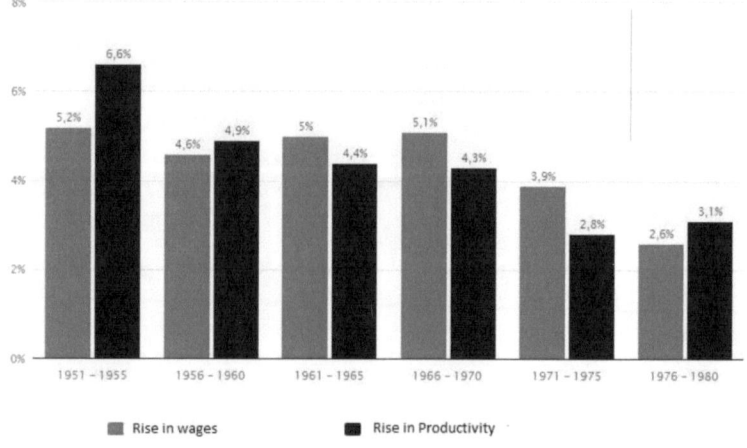

Figure 4 (Federal Statistics Office, 2013 data)

Gesamtentwicklung des deutschen Außenhandels in Millionen Euro

Jahr [1]	Tatsächliche Werte		Ausfuhr (+) bzw. Einfuhrüberschuss (-)	Zu- / Abnahme gegenüber Vorjahr in Prozent	
	Ausfuhr	Einfuhr		Ausfuhr	Einfuhr
1950	4 275	5 815	- 1 540		
1951	7 453	7 529	- 76	+ 74,3	+ 29,5
1952	8 645	8 284	+ 361	+ 16,0	+ 10,0
1953	9 472	8 186	+ 1 286	+ 9,6	- 1,2
1954	11 266	9 887	+ 1 379	+ 18,9	+ 20,8
1955	13 149	12 512	+ 637	+ 16,7	+ 26,6
1956	15 779	14 298	+ 1 481	+ 20,0	+ 14,3
1957	18 390	16 206	+ 2 184	+ 16,5	+ 13,3
1958	18 917	15 918	+ 2 999	+ 2,9	- 1,8
1959	21 057	18 316	+ 2 741	+ 11,3	+ 15,1
1960	24 514	21 844	+ 2 670	+ 16,4	+ 19,3
1961	26 065	22 682	+ 3 383	+ 6,3	+ 3,8
1962	27 086	25 308	+ 1 778	+ 3,9	+ 11,6
1963	29 813	26 729	+ 3 084	+ 10,1	+ 5,6
1964	33 193	30 084	+ 3 109	+ 11,3	+ 12,6
1965	36 635	36 019	+ 616	+ 10,4	+ 19,7
1966	41 224	37 156	+ 4 068	+ 12,5	+ 3,2
1967	44 505	35 884	+ 8 621	+ 8,0	- 3,4
1968	50 900	41 506	+ 9 394	+ 14,4	+ 15,7
1969	58 061	50 092	+ 7 969	+ 14,1	+ 20,7
1970	64 053	56 041	+ 8 012	+ 10,3	+ 11,9
1971	69 541	61 416	+ 8 125	+ 8,6	+ 9,6
1972	76 194	65 826	+ 10 368	+ 9,6	+ 7,2
1973	91 212	74 351	+ 16 861	+ 19,7	+ 13,0
1974	117 893	91 896	+ 25 997	+ 29,3	+ 23,6
1975	113 297	94 238	+ 19 059	- 3,9	+ 2,5
1976	131 219	113 595	+ 17 624	+ 15,8	+ 20,5
1977	139 897	120 245	+ 19 652	+ 6,6	+ 5,9
1978	145 671	124 605	+ 21 066	+ 4,1	+ 3,6
1979	160 785	149 318	+ 11 467	+ 10,4	+ 19,8
1980	179 120	174 545	+ 4 575	+ 11,4	+ 16,9
1981	202 931	188 758	+ 14 173	+ 13,3	+ 8,1
1982	218 701	192 483	+ 26 218	+ 7,8	+ 2,0
1983	221 022	199 502	+ 21 520	+ 1,1	+ 3,6
1984	249 624	222 032	+ 27 592	+ 12,9	+ 11,3
1985	274 648	237 143	+ 37 505	+ 10,0	+ 6,8
1986	269 125	211 544	+ 57 581	- 2,0	- 10,8
1987	269 644	209 446	+ 60 198	+ 0,2	- 1,0
1988	290 237	224 769	+ 65 468	+ 7,6	+ 7,3
1989	327 759	258 951	+ 68 808	+ 12,9	+ 15,2
1990	348 117	293 215	+ 54 902	+ 6,2	+ 13,2
1991	340 425	329 228	+ 11 197	- 2,2	+ 12,3
1992	343 089	325 972	+ 17 117	+ 0,8	- 1,0
1993	321 289	289 644	+ 31 645	- 6,4	- 11,1
1994	353 084	315 444	+ 37 640	+ 9,9	+ 8,9
1995	383 232	339 617	+ 43 615	+ 8,5	+ 7,7
1996	403 377	352 995	+ 50 382	+ 5,3	+ 3,9
1997	454 342	394 794	+ 59 548	+ 12,6	+ 11,8
1998	488 371	423 452	+ 64 919	+ 7,5	+ 7,3
1999	510 008	444 797	+ 65 211	+ 4,4	+ 5,0
2000	597 440	538 311	+ 59 129	+ 17,1	+ 21,0
2001	638 268	542 774	+ 95 494	+ 6,8	+ 0,8
2002	651 320	518 532	+ 132 788	+ 2,0	- 4,5
2003	664 455	534 534	+ 129 921	+ 2,0	+ 3,1
2004	731 544	575 448	+ 156 096	+ 10,1	+ 7,7
2005	786 266	628 087	+ 158 179	+ 7,5	+ 9,1
2006	893 042	733 994	+ 159 048	+ 13,6	+ 16,9
2007	965 236	769 887	+ 195 349	+ 8,1	+ 4,9
2008	984 140	805 842	+ 178 298	+ 2,0	+ 4,7
2009	803 312	664 615	+ 138 697	- 18,4	- 17,5
2010	951 959	797 097	+ 154 863	+ 18,5	+ 19,9
2011	1 061 225	902 523	+ 158 702	+ 11,5	+ 13,2
2012	1 095 766	905 925	+ 189 841	+ 3,3	+ 0,4
2013	1 093 115	898 164	+ 194 951	- 0,2	- 0,9

1) 1950 bis 1989: Gebietsstand bis zum 3. Oktober 1990
Ab 1990: Gebietsstand ab dem 3. Oktober 1990

Figure 5 (Economic Growth , Jones, Vollrath, Textbook, 2014)

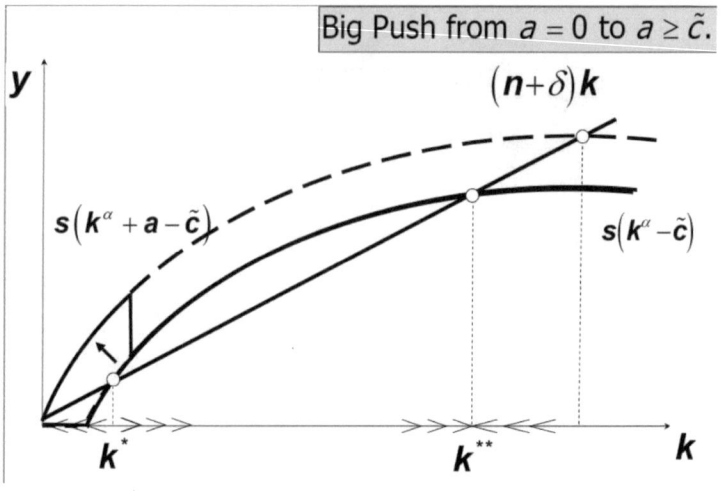

Appendix:

1 – The Data Table used for the Essay was Madison table. There was a slight difference of some data between Madison Table and Federal Statistics Table, especially with Population between 1946 and 1955. The Madison Table does not reflect the population growth in high scale whereas other reliable sources mention that, few years after the war, the inflow of returning soldiers and other refugees were over 6 million.

2- It is assumed that the Investment in Germany came from within as there is no time series data available about the Foreign Direct Investment (FDI) from 1950 to 1974.

3- Refugees to Germany mainly included the German citizens who previously lived in other countries of Europe or in places occupied by Germany who immigrated to Germany fearing the revenge due to atrocities committed by the Nazis during World War II. Similarly, there were agreements to exchange war prisoners who eventually returned to Germany in the coming decades.

4 –With the law ' Rights to Return ',partners, children and grandchildren of German soldiers who settled in various parts of the Soviet Union gained the right to live in Germany. The total number of immigrants[1]

5 – The Basic Solow Model with Human Capital can be written as: $Y = K^{\alpha} (AH)^{1-\alpha}$

6 – Output per worker in a steady state can be given by: $y^*(t) = \left(\frac{sk}{n+g+d}\right)^{\alpha/(1-\alpha)} hA(t)$

---

[1] Muenz, Ulrich, Changing Patterns of Immigration to Germany, University of Berlin, https://migration.ucdavis.edu/rs/more.php?id=69_0_3_0 Retrieved 18th Nov 2014

References

Castillo Daniel, 'German Economy in the 1920s'. University of California, Santa Barbara. 2003 http://www.history.ucsb.edu/faculty/marcuse/classes/33d/projects/1920s/Econ20s.htm . Retrieved on 9th Nov 2014

Smolny Werner, 'Post-war growth, productivity convergence and reconstruction': A theoretical and empirical investigation. University of Konstanz, Germany, June 1999. http://www.ruhr-uni-bochum.de/agvwp1/dl2/waox3.pdf . Retrieved on 9th November 2014.

Oltmer, Jochen, ' Zwangswanderungen nach dem zweiten Weltkrieg ' (Translation: Forced Migration after World War II) Migration Basics, Center for Political Education, 2005.
http://www.bpb.de/themen/CNSEUC,0,0,Zwangswanderungen_nach_dem_Zweiten_Weltkrieg.html . Retrieved 15th Nov 2014

Borowsky Peter, ' Das Ende der Ara Adenauer ' (Translation: The End of Adenauer Era), 2002, Center for Political Education . http://www.bpb.de/izpb/10093/das-ende-der-aera-adenauer?p=all. Retrieved 15th Nov 2014

Eichengreen Barry ' Understanding West German Economic Growth in the 1950s ', Discussion Paper on Economic Risk, Berlin, 2008. http://sfb649.wiwi.hu-berlin.de/papers/pdf/SFB649DP2008-068.pdf . Retrieved 15th Nov 2014

Federal Statistical Department Data
https://www.destatis.de/DE/ZahlenFakten/Indikatoren/LangeReihen/Arbeitsmarkt/lrerw013.html. Retrieved 10th Nov 2014

Williamson Samuel, ' Seven Ways to Compute the Relative Value of a US Dollar Amount, 1774 to present, ' MeasuringWorth, 2014. Taken via http://www.measuringworth.com/uscompare/ , Retrieved 11th Nov 2014.

Abelshauser Werner, The Dynamics of German Industry: Germany's Path Toward the New Economy and the American Challenge, October 2005, ISBN 978-1-84545-072-4 . Gained Access through Glasgow University Online Services via http://www.jstor.org/stable/29770469?seq=3 . Retrieved 11th Nov 2014.

Daron Acemoglu, Simon Johnson, James Robinson, 'Institutions as a fundamental cause of long-run growth', Handbook of Economic Growth, Volume IA, 2005. http://economics.mit.edu/files/4469 Retrieved: 11th Nov 2014

Detzer Daniel, Nina Dodig, Trevor Evans, Eckhard Hein, Hansjorg Herr, ' The German Financial System ' Institute for International Political Economy, Berlin School of Economics and Law. 2013. http://www.fessud.eu/wp-content/uploads/PDF/German%20Financial%20System%20-%20Final%2015.05.2013.pdf Retrieved on 12th Nov 2014

Simpson C.V. J , ' The German Sparkassen: A Commentary and Case Study ' Page 32, Civitas 2013, London . ISBN 978-1-906837-46-4 . http://www.civitas.org.uk/economy/SimpsonSparkassen.pdf . Retrieved 11th Nov 2014

Wendy Carlin, University College London Paper, ' West German Growth and Institutions, 1945 – 90', http://www.ucl.ac.uk/~uctpa36/west%20germany%20in%20crafts%20toniolo.pdf . Retrieved on 12th Nov 2014

Haupt Reinhard, ' Vom Wirtschaftswunder zur Wirtschaftskrise – Ursachen und Folgen des Werteverfalls ' (Translation: From Economic Miracle to Economic Crisis –Causes and Consequences of the fall of Value) , Institute of Science and Belief, 2014.
http://www.iguw.de/uploads/media/wirtsch_wunder.pdf Retrieved: 11th Nov 2014

Keynes, John Maynard, 'Economic Consequences of the Peace', 1920. Chapter: Reparation. New York, Harcourt, Brace Howe Inc.

YOUR KNOWLEDGE HAS VALUE

- We will publish your bachelor's and master's thesis, essays and papers

- Your own eBook and book -
  sold worldwide in all relevant shops

- Earn money with each sale

Upload your text at www.GRIN.com
and publish for free